BRUTAL TRUTH

Unfiltered talk. Unfluffy wisdom.

by Damian Mason

BRUTAL TRUTH

Unfiltered talk. Unfluffy wisdom.

by Damian Mason

Published by:
Boy on a Bike Publishing

www.DamianMason.com
888-304-0702

Printed in the United States of America.
ISBN: 978-1-4951-9538-9

A NOTE ABOUT QUOTES

This is a collection of my quotes and statements.

There's a very good chance some of this unfiltered talk and unfluffy wisdom will resonate with you.

Post these quotes on your mirror or bulletin board for daily motivation. Share them with a friend in need of some truth. And by all means, share them on social media. But if you do, please give credit where credit is due.

Talking and writing is my business. Shakespeare it ain't, but it's still my material and it IS copyrighted. And frankly, it's a hell of a lot more practical than a bunch of "wherefore art thous" written by an English guy in tights!

#BrutalTruth by Damian Mason

If you believe success and happiness are self made, this book is for you. But if you don't believe you control your own destiny, this book is especially for you — obviously you need to be enlightened.

This book is straight talk about life, success, business, prosperity, fulfillment, and happiness.

If you're looking for feel good fiction with happy endings, watch a Disney movie.

Contrary to what some people believe, tonight while you're eating junk food and watching dumbed down TV, a unicorn isn't going to show up in a magical flash and haul you to the "life you deserve."

NEWSFLASH!
You ARE living the life you deserve. That's the truth.

There is no pixie dust. There is no secret to success. And, aside from the government sanctioned lottery, which preys on the mathematical ignorance of the masses, there is no "get rich quick" option.

The gullible have paid billions of dollars to charlatans telling them otherwise. I won't do that. In the pages that follow, I'm giving you credit as an intelligent, driven individual who seeks a better life and business. Sure, you can find *rah rah* motivational types and snake oil salesmen who'll take your money, telling you your failures aren't your fault and "anything is possible," but you won't find that here.

Achievement, prosperity, and happiness are all possible. But you won't get there by reading 7 generic habits, being "passionate," or sitting in a sweat lodge.

I'm not being mean, I'm being honest. If it's too harsh for your delicate disposition, check out the children's book section. Fairy tales are for kids, this book is for adults.

Life is about choices and results. Life IS black and white. Stop making excuses.

THIS IS THE BRUTAL TRUTH.

DEDICATION

*This book is dedicated to the
precious few who possess the balls
to speak the truth, and to those
with the strength to hear the truth.*

I'd like you to read this whole book
from cover to cover. However, if
you're the "ADHD — cut to the
chase — I have a short attention
span and I didn't take my meds"
type, here are the sections.

Go ahead, turn to the category that
suits you best and dig in!

BUSINESS

GOALS

LIFE

MONEY

MOTIVATION

PEOPLE

SUCCESS

WORK ETHIC

REINVENTION

BUSINESS

President Kennedy once said, "My father always told me that all businessmen were sons of bitches." That statement is so telling of how little regard — contempt even — the political class has for private enterprise.

I much prefer the quote of another former president, Calvin Coolidge, who said:,"The chief business of the American people is business."

I love business. That's why I made it chapter one.

Business is trade, commerce, production, and all the things that separate us from the animals.

Much as the anti-capitalism crowd bemoans profits, to date we've yet to find a cure for human self-interest.

Therein lies the beauty and simplicity of business. You produce a good or service and deliver it to the marketplace; the marketplace determines its value.

That's business. Want to improve upon your business skills? Read on!

A sale isn't a sale until you get paid.

There's no such thing as self-employed — you can't

pay yourself until someone else pays you first.

Customers don't pay for your talent.

They pay for the value your talent delivers to them.

BUSINESS

Ideas are easy; implementing them is hard.

If your only sales tactic is to be low priced,

your employer should fire you and replace you

with a price sheet.

There's no such thing as "the perfect time"

or "the right economy" to launch your

business venture.

Clients and customers care about themselves.

Don't make your problem their problem.

Bad customers and bad employees should both

be fired. They interfere with your ability

to serve your good clientele.

Five keys to entrepreneurial success:

drive, financial savvy, creativity,

risk tolerance, and salesmanship.

Every job is paid training for the next one.

Sales is understanding a customer's need,

then positioning yourself as the solution.

Don't take advice from someone who has never

done what they're advising you to do.

A SALE IS ONLY A SALE IF YOU GET PAID; OTHERWISE, IT'S A GIFT.

The quality of your product or service is meaningless if it doesn't have an application in a customer's life or business.

"Non Profit" status with the IRS doesn't mean there isn't a whole lot of money being made by the cause.

Telling people what they want to hear can be very profitable.

In business, don't make it difficult
for people to give you money.

Unless you're the local utility, you needn't sell
something to every person at every address.
Fortunes have been made selling to a very small
percentage of the marketplace.

It doesn't take talent to return calls,
show up on time, and be responsible.

YOU NEVER WIN BY BEING THE CHEAPEST BECAUSE THERE'S ALWAYS SOME IDIOT WILLING TO DO IT CHEAPER THAN YOU.

People complain that they're in a "competitive business." NEWS FLASH! They're all competitive businesses.

Never sell what you cannot deliver.

Show me what your product does, and I'm interested. Show me what your product does FOR ME, and I'm a buyer.

In business, you should sell what people want, not what you can make.

When you take action on principle, be very clear about what the principle is worth to you.

Trends come and go but business basics like quality, salesmanship, and taking care of the customer never go out of style.

Business has two modes: Survive and Thrive.

Long term prosperity can never be attained by a

business stuck in a survival mentality.

Respect and wealth are both earned.

Question the motive and the honesty of anyone

who prefaces a business transaction by saying,

"I'm not making any money on this."

Regardless of occupation,

we ALL work for other people.

When you tolerate disrespect and mistreatment

from those you deal with, you promote more

disrespect and mistreatment.

"Word of Mouth" is an insult to the established

business. Long-term success is derived from

"Word of Reputation."

GOALS

Real change requires clarifying priorities. Goals do that. Goals focus your objective and guide your daily activity.

Goals are specific results you want to achieve. To be effective or "self-enforceable," they should have a timetable.

So instead of just talking about what you'd "like" to achieve, be proactive. Set your goals, write them down, and look at them several times per week to keep yourself on track.

Need help setting goals? Write down 3 categories: Personal, Business, and Financial. Under each category identify a short-term, mid-term, and long-term objective. For example: have one "date night" per week with your spouse, change jobs by the end of the year, have $100,000 invested within 5 years.

See how easy that was? Now make it happen!

Never get so caught up in the process of doing something that you lose sight of what that something was supposed to accomplish.

Goals are more important than business plans.

Saying you're goal-oriented would be more believable if you actually set and achieved goals.

If you don't have a goal, how will you know

what you're trying to accomplish?

You can always come up with an excuse.

New years resolutions don't fail;

the people who make them do.

Failures make excuses, achievers make goals.

Problems don't get fixed by
pretending they don't exist.

Keep doing what you've always done, and you'll
keep getting what you've always gotten — unless
your competition adapts to what you've always
done, in which case you may get nothing.

Remarkably, almost no positive outcome ever
resulted from a midnight toast of champagne.
Positive change requires work.

RESOLUTIONS ARE IDLE JANUARY STATEMENTS IF YOU CAN'T SEE THE RESULTS BY JUNE.

We are all given an equal amount of time each day to better ourselves.

Newsflash: You ARE doing what you WANT to be doing, otherwise you'd make a change.

Just because you want more for others doesn't mean they do.

New year's resolutions for most people are about as effective as birthday wishes, because the same amount of effort goes into each. Real change requires more than blowing out a candle and eating cake.

Resolving to do things differently in the new year is a good start. Actually doing things differently is even better.

Write down your resolutions and look at them daily as a "To-Do" list for a better life.

LIFE

There are two ways to travel through life: As a pilot, or as a passenger.

Being a pilot requires training, responsibility, and effort. The benefits: you're in charge of where you go, when to stop, how fast you move, how high you fly, and how long you spend at each destination.

Being a passenger is easier. You don't have to make any decisions. Eventually you'll end up somewhere. No responsibilities, no effort, all you have to do is show up and sit.

This might sound simplistic, but think of the people you know who bitch about their life's destination as though it was imposed on them.

Life's a fantastic journey (with occasional turbulence). Do you want to be in the cockpit charting the course, or in seat 22E hoping to end up somewhere pleasant?

You can run from your past,

but you can't hide from yourself.

Beer may not necessarily make me smarter, but it

does help me tolerate those who are dumber.

Don't be the company that misery loves to keep.

Life is to be lived, not tolerated.

Life is about decision making.

Decide if you want to be financially solvent

and happy, or broke and unhappy.

If you accept it, you endorse it.

When did "compassion" become:

taking money from responsible people

and handing it over to the irresponsible?

If you can't be good, at least be memorable!

Sometimes "the going gets tough"

because you're doing it wrong.

When you long for the good old days, do yourself

a favor and remember the bad old days too.

LIFE

31

THE BEST ADVICE I COULD EVER GIVE: BE CAREFUL OF WHO YOU CHOOSE TO TAKE ADVICE FROM.

I can make you laugh,

but I can't make you happy.

Recipe for a successful comedy show:

a well illuminated presenter and

an audience that's half lit!

Hardest part of comedy? Tolerating

unfunny people who think they are.

The internet hasn't made people smarter, but it has made it easier for dumb people to group up.

It's true, birds of a feather do flock together. So who are you flying with?

You're probably devoting concern and energy to items of very little consequence.

Character is the most important consideration

in business and personal relationships.

LIFE

Coming home to an unhappy personal life

with a big paycheck still requires coming home

to an unhappy personal life.

In life and in business there is

risk and reward. Period.

Government might be efficient

if it had competitors.

If stress were a nosebleed,

would you manage it or stop it?

When someone is wrong, have the backbone

to disagree; and don't soften your position by

opening your statement with, "I'm sorry, but…"

YOU HAVE THE RIGHT TO PURSUE YOUR DREAMS, BUT THERE'S NO GUARANTEE YOU'LL BE COMPENSATED FOR IT.

Documenting your back yard chickens on Facebook doesn't constitute "dropping off the grid."

What keeps you up at night is very likely the things you should have handled during the day.

Losing will teach you more lessons than winning, if you are smart enough to learn from the process of losing.

An excuse is a smokescreen used

to cover a lack of desire.

Your feelings don't trump my rights.

Whoever said "getting there is half the fun"

never went anywhere. And if they did, they

didn't fly through Chicago O'Hare.

THERE'S NO SPECIAL AWARD FOR DOING EVERYTHING THE HARD WAY.

You won't always enjoy the people you do business with, but eventually you should do business with people you like. It's less stressful.

Nothing brings fresh perspective to a problem like a little distance.

Favor a weak muscle, and the strong muscles around it get stronger to compensate, while the weak muscle atrophies and becomes weaker. The same thing happens when you favor weak humans.

Spend your life chasing only money and status and you'll likely end up with neither.

How bad does an airline have to be to go out of business? Even the ones that are in business suck!

Spend your days maximizing life, and you won't have time to worry about death.

Aside from inheritance, wealth is attained through earning, saving, and investing.

Want money? Maximize your earnings. Sounds simple, but lots of people who complain about money problems have an amazing amount of spare time.

Let's assume you are an income maximizer. Good for you. How are your saving and investing habits?

I remember a stat from a college finance class that I've never forgotten. In a poll, most people stated that if they just earned an additional $5,000 of income, they'd devote more to savings, debt mitigation, and investments.

Remarkably, that answer was the same for those earning $20,000 per year and for those earning $200,000 annually.

Point: Most people spend everything they earn, regardless of income.

You've done the hard work of earning money, now do the easy work of saving it. Wealth is about discipline, not lucky breaks.

Money is not the root of all evil, unscrupulous people are. Money is merely a system of exchange.

Sometimes you need to spend money to make money, but there is a difference between spending and investing.

When you've sacrificed personal happiness and your sense of humor for money, you've paid a very high price.

Poor choices = Poorness

People who say "money's not important to me"

typically don't have money, but they're

happy to use yours.

MONEY

A low-return investment is still an investment,

and that's more than most people possess.

A lot of money is spent on kid's sports under the misguided parental premise of pursuing an athletic scholarship.

Money can't buy happiness, but it can buy personal freedom and independence.

Contrary to what you've convinced yourself, giving your adult children money doesn't help them.

Earning, saving, and investing

are all teachable activities.

You don't need a degree in finance

to live below your means.

Wealth is a habit that becomes a lifestyle.

Working hard to earn money but not investing any of it is sort of like running the first 26 miles of a marathon, then quitting without finishing the .2.

Nobody owes you anything.

Don't pretend money is the answer to everything; there are lots of problems money can't fix!

IF YOU'RE LIVING "PAYCHECK TO PAYCHECK" YOU'RE LIVING BEYOND YOUR MEANS.

Money won't buy fulfillment.

Being poor because of a lifetime of bad decisions

doesn't constitute "unfairness."

Ultimately, people earn what they're worth.

(With the exception of federal government

employees who are over compensated.)

Financial excuses: I know someone who's been broke since 1995 due to the recession of 2008.

Approximately 10% of failures that are blamed on the economy are actually due to a bad economy.

MONEY

Wanna fix unemployment?

Stop paying people to be unemployed.

Taxing people for earning income is like disciplining children for being good.

Debt is a daily obligation to an individual or institution. So how obligated do you want to be?

Using consumer credit to finance a lifestyle creates a lifestyle of indebtedness.

Most "money" problems are actually decision making problems.

Ever notice there are no rich people standing in line to buy lottery tickets?

Your employer sets your income, but you control your expenditures.

IF YOU DON'T HAVE MONEY FOR SAVING OR INVESTING NOW, WHEN WILL YOU?

Economics, at its core, is not about charts, graphs, or supply and demand curves. It's about human decision-making.

Propping up your irresponsible children isn't "being a good parent," it's being an enabler.

All the physical possessions in the world won't fulfill a miserable person.

Your financial problems are

not your employer's fault.

People do what they are compensated

to do, be it work or welfare.

Every financially overextended person has an

excuse, but somehow it's never the person

swiping their credit card that's to blame.

MOTIVATION

This section might inspire you. Then again, it may not. That's the way motivation works — it's different for every personality type.

Some people need a hug, others need a drill sergeant. Some people respond to money, others require accolades. It's the age old question of carrot versus stick. Truth is, most people need both.

Frankly, motivation boils down to this: You're either driven, or you're not. If you've never pushed yourself to accomplish something, this book won't change you.

This chapter is for those of you who ARE driven, who DO want more. Because sometimes even overachievers need a kick in the pants!

There is no Santa Claus;

your wishes are your responsibility.

"Can't" is a very powerful word.

Debilitatingly powerful, in fact.

The list of things you are truly incapable of doing

is about one tenth as long as the list

of things you say you can't do.

"Brilliant" is good, but "responsible" is better.

A lifetime of laziness, irresponsibility, and poor

choices does not constitute "bad luck."

Exercise equipment, like every other tool,

is useless without human effort.

You'll never up your game if you keep playing at the kiddie table.

Ambition trumps brains.

There are plenty of lazy smart people.

Misery loves company because it's easier to find people to commiserate with than to get off one's ass and actually change the situation.

ANOTHER PERSON'S JOB MIGHT LOOK EASY FROM YOUR ANGLE, BUT REMEMBER: WORK IS WORK.

What time you wake up is meaningless;

it's what you do while you're awake that matters.

Opportunity knocks, but it doesn't kick in the

door, stroll into the living room, flop down on the

couch next to your unmotivated self, and make

you successful.

Talent is meaningless if you can't

perform when the spotlight is on you.

You'll die waiting for the "perfect business opportunity" to come along.

Your unwillingness to educate yourself on a subject doesn't make me wrong.

A motivational speaker, standing on a stage talking, can not change your life. But you can.

Most "natural talent" got that way
through lots of practice.

If entrepreneurs took all the "cautionary advice"
bankers, lawyers, and accountants offered,
we'd still be in the dark ages.

Acceptance of laziness and underachievement
doesn't mean you're patient, it just means
you have low standards.

Accomplishment is derived from doing,

not talking about doing.

Excuses are easy, results are difficult

At some point you have all the data you need,

it's a matter of pulling the trigger.

SAYING YOU WANT SOMETHING TO HAPPEN WON'T MAKE IT HAPPEN.

If it's important to you, you'll do it.

The reward for playing the victim is sympathy.

Do you want people to feel sorry for you?

Thinking about it and talking

about it are not DOING it.

Comedy is like being a designated hitter in baseball. For that brief time, when all eyes are on you, you gotta hit!

You're not someone else's responsibility.

Blaming others for your failures doesn't erase the failure.

Eventually you run out of "somedays."

Stop procrastinating.

There is no trying. There is only

doing and not doing.

Don't use your past to justify your present

or determine your future.

Worry is natural. Taking action

to alleviate worry isn't.

What's stressing you out today is stuff

you know you should have addressed yesterday.

Do you want to spend your golden years

regretting the chances you didn't take?

JUST BECAUSE YOU DON'T LIKE WHAT YOU HEAR, THAT DOESN'T MAKE IT WRONG.

There are no such things as "super foods,"
"cleanses," or miracle diets. There are, however:
healthy eating, portion control,
and sweat by exercise.

When you protect your kids from work and
failing, what are you really teaching them?

Just because your bad choices didn't kill you,
that's no reason to continue making bad choices.

Fear is probably your biggest limiting factor.

A rut is only a rut if it's temporary;

otherwise, it's your life.

If your reason for anything is: "It's not fair,"

formulate a better reason.

Don't let years make you complacent.

You can always get better.

Despite what Oprah says, being passionate

about a subject isn't going to

make you successful.

When *rah rah* motivational types tell you you can

be anything in life, they're lying. You can be a lot

of things, but you can't be anything.

Do today what you know is the right thing to do,

or you'll spend your retirement years

regretting that you didn't.

Don't confuse a lack of balls and

backbone for "caution."

In life, work, and show business, the time comes when preparation and practice are over and it's time to perform!

Some folks are willing to pay for bad advice, as long as it agrees with what they already believe.

Think like the rest of the crowd, and you'll get lost in the crowd.

PEOPLE (LIE)

We're told "honesty is the best policy." Yet, the more you deal with humans the more obvious it becomes that most of them never received the policy book.

Honesty gets you sued, fired, reprimanded, or at the very least, labeled.

So people lie.

"You're not fat, those images on TV are unrealistic." "You didn't fail, the economy was bad." "You never had the right opportunity." "It's not your fault." "That's a great idea, boss." "You're not lazy, you're just bored." Blah blah blah.

People even lie to themselves to justify their situation. "I'm too busy." "I don't have time." "I don't earn enough money to invest." "I'd like to make a career change, but...."

Everyone has an excuse. The more convincing the lie, the more valid their excuse.

The best self help advice I can give you:

Stop lying to others and stop lying to yourself.

You'll sleep better knowing you conduct your business and live your life with integrity.

In the contest over who has it worse,

there is no winner.

Peer pressure is only bad if your peers are.

Insecurity oftentimes masks itself as arrogance.

Rationalizing your situation won't change it.

Hanging around dumb people might make you

feel smart, but it seldom makes you feel good.

Many people confuse dishonesty with niceness.

Emotions: they separate us from the animals

and cause us to make really bad decisions.

"I'll try" is what weak people say

when they really mean "no."

When you tell others about your problems,

are you seeking sympathy, or a lower

standard of acceptability?

For most people, saying what they actually mean

is a second language they don't speak fluently.

People care about themselves. Your interests

are a secondary consideration.

Lots of people go through life faking it.

Sometimes people do what's right. Usually they

do what they can get away with.

RESPECT THE PERSON WHO CAN OUTSMART YOU, BUT FEAR THE PERSON WHO CAN OUT-DUMB YOU!

Fear of confrontation doesn't remove stress, it creates it.

People don't wake up every morning thinking of ways to benefit you; they're thinking about themselves.

Lots of people are convinced their child is gifted. Some actually are.

The weak prefer you lie to them;

strong people want the truth.

People conveniently forget the decision they

made 20 years ago that put them in

the situation they're in today.

There are people determined to hold you back.

Some of them are disguised as friends.

Some individuals are difficult to deal with because they're fighting a battle you weren't even aware you were fighting.

Lots of people fear the decision more than the outcome.

Being offended doesn't entitle you to compensation.

A prevailing negative mindset is more harmful

than years of recession.

People who walk through life focused on events

behind them tend to fall down.

Failures enjoy seeing others fail.

It gives them legitimacy.

NOBODY CARES ABOUT YOUR PROBLEM UNLESS IT IMPACTS THEM.

Never underestimate the fragility and emotional instability of those you deal with.

If you and your friends gossip about other people when you get together, what do you suppose they do when you're not around?

Those attempting to make you feel guilty for what you have, want what you have.

Humans are human, which means they're typically ruled by emotion, not logic.

Hanging around bitter, jaded, judgmental people will likely make you bitter, jaded, and judgmental. So why do it?

PEOPLE

The biggest impediment to communication for most people is an inability to listen.

LEARN FROM THE FAILURE OF OTHERS, BUT NOT FROM THOSE WHO DWELL ON THEIR FAILURES.

People don't respect what they pity.

There are three kinds of people: Those who make things happen, those who watch things happen, and those who wonder what happened.

People don't always agree or work together mindlessly without question. If we did, we'd be an ant colony.

In life there are players, spectators, and people outside the stadium unaware that a game is going on. Which one are you?

Always beware the person
who has less to lose than you do.

Sometimes the crowd listens to the most qualified person, but usually they listen to the loudest.

SUCCESS

You're probably wasting time on things that don't matter and won't make you successful.

A perfectly crafted business plan will not make you successful. Neither will a nicely worded corporate mission statement. You see, success is mostly about doing, not talking about doing. Which is what most business plans and mission statements end up being — just talk.

Humans love to procrastinate under the guise of "planning" because, let's face it, "doing" takes effort. More importantly, success involves risk, and most people have no stomach for risk.

So they plan, and contemplate, and deliberate, then ultimately decide "this wasn't the right opportunity."

Understand this: There is no right time, perfect economy, or golden opportunity. There's just commitment, and action toward achieving a goal. That's the "secret" to success.

Prosperity tomorrow requires

a few sacrifices today.

When critics refer to someone as an "overnight

success," they're right: the prosperous one's

success occurred while the critic was sleeping.

Don't apologize for being successful.

WHEN APPROACHING ANY SITUATION, CLARIFY THE OUTCOME YOU DESIRE.

There's no guilt when you've earned everything you have.

There's an endless line of people willing to make excuses for the weak and under accomplished, whereas the strong and successful have a line of critics.

Busy isn't the same as productive.

Underachievers take the easiest

option in life, then justify their decision.

Ever notice, those who blame everything on bad

luck always seem to have bad luck?

The secret to success is that there is no secret.

There is, however, effort, commitment,

creativity, and risk-taking.

SUCCESS IS 10% ABOUT THE IDEA, AND 90% ABOUT EXECUTING IT.

Nothing drives your detractors crazier than your continued prosperity and happiness.

Saying you're unhealthy, broke, and unhappy because that's "just the way it was meant to be" is a poverty mindset.

Just about every person will tell you they want to improve themselves; very few of them will actually do it.

SUCCESS

Don't measure activity,

measure accomplishment.

Lots of people devote time and energy to trivial

matters because they're afraid to tackle the

really important stuff.

Some people hate others for their success

because it reminds them of their own failure.

WORK ETHIC

I've met a lot of successful people, but I've yet to meet one who didn't work.

I'm not talking about the trust fund crowd burning through grandpa's inheritance. Those people aren't successful, they're private welfare cases. And if you've been around enough trust fund types, you understand why you should never give your offspring money — it makes them lazy.

I'm talking about work ethic as it pertains to you and me, who actually earn our money.

Education is important. As is talent, training, and skill. But until your skills, smarts, and talent deliver value to a paying customer, it's all for naught. That's where work ethic comes in.

Some people are good at whatever task you give them. Not because of talent or aptitude, but because of work ethic and responsibility. Remember those two characteristics the next time you hire people.

Training won't necessarily make you good at anything. But training and commitment can make you good at lots of things.

It's trendy to talk about "finding one's passion," but lots of people just need to find a work ethic.

Ever notice the amount of effort people put into something meaningless in an effort to avoid important stuff that they're afraid to take on because it involves effort?

Underachievers love to say what they "could have done."

WORK ETHIC

WISDOM COMES FROM EXPERIENCE. EXPERIENCE COMES FROM DOING SOMETHING. UNDERSTAND?

Ask the guy who's good at doing chin ups

if he got that way through natural talent

or by doing chin ups.

Incompetence is more a lack of

desire than a lack of ability.

Productivity breeds productivity.

WORK ETHIC

Sure, work can be enjoyable, but above all, work

has to produce value — otherwise, it's a pastime.

Showbiz success requires work and talent.

The talent lies in making it look like it isn't work.

Unwillingness to work is not a disability.

You have two choices: You can sit around waiting

for your lucky break, or you can take proactive

steps today that will reap benefits tomorrow.

Perfect attendance is more important in life

than honor roll. You gotta show up!

Chances are, it's not a lack of talent

that's limiting your prosperity.

WORK ETHIC

REINVENTION

If the old saying is true, "the only thing constant is change," why would you be an exception? Answer: you're not!

Success and longevity are achieved by REINVENTING yourself, your brand, and your business.

The marketplace WILL be different tomorrow. Will you evolve to remain relevant? Even if you've had tremendous personal or business success, transformation is necessary. Why? Because the world sees you as you were, not as you want to be. You're pigeonholed!

Most people don't like change. But stagnation is slow death.

Start your REINVENTION with this:

1. Describe yourself, your brand, or your business in one sentence.

2. What are the problems with how you are currently viewed / branded?

3. What specific tasks can you undertake to evolve positively from where you are today and where you want to be?

4. What benefits are to be attained through REINVENTING yourself?

Remember, you adapt to survive. But you REINVENT to thrive!

If the only thing constant is change,

why would your business be any different?

REINVENT: Verb.

1. The act of staying relevant in an ever-
changing, competitive marketplace.

2. Altering your product or image to
succeed in business.

In nature and in business you have

two choices: evolution or extinction.

REINVENTION

Want to be green? Recycle.
Want to be successful? REINVENT!

You're right. Your brand is unique, your product is amazing, and no company or person could ever compete with you. Don't change a thing. Ever. (That's sarcasm and if you recognize that, you probably also recognize the need to REINVENT for business success.)

The Yellow Pages and the morning newspaper were once revolutionary business ideas. The marketplace keeps changing. Do you?

You survive by adapting to your environment.
You thrive by adapting to your environment
better than your competition.

Bubble Wrap was originally designed to be
wallpaper. Then greenhouse insulation. It took two
failures, two REINVENTIONS, and several years
before Bubble Wrap became packing material.

Business is good, so why make any changes,
right? Because your competition is.

REINVENTION

If you're in a rut, make yourself a little bit uncomfortable, and you'll be amazed at how creative you become.

Nobody cares what you used to be!

Once upon a time, Kodak, Blockbuster, and Pan Am were successful busiesses too....

FOCUSING ON YOUR COMPETITION IS REACTING. FOCUSING ON THE FUTURE IS REINVENTING.

Re-create yourself in the eyes of your customers, or become a commodity in the eyes of your customers. Commodities are sold on price; unique products are sold on value proposition. Want to make more money? Avoid becoming a commodity.

Success can spawn from one good idea, but longevity requires constant creativity.

Market followers obsess over their competitors. Market leaders look at how their product fits into the future.

Three ways to REINVENT your business:
change your product, change your customers,
or change your image.

To advance, you must be willing to grow out
of or even sever existing relationships, be they
professional or personal.

Don't be afraid to discard old ideas;
it creates room for new ones!

REINVENTION

BUSINESSES FAIL DUE TO LACK OF INNOVATION BUT BLAME THEIR FAILURE ON COMPETITION.

The more established you and your business are, the more difficult it is to REINVENT — Your customers have you pigeonholed.

The time to REINVENT yourself, your brand, and your business is before it becomes necessary.

REINVENTING your brand requires more than a "new and improved" label.

REINVENTION

Wal-Mart started selling groceries.
Ford reinvented the F-150. If you think you're
too successful to change, think again.

Marlboros were a faltering brand marketed
to ladies. Then came the Marlboro Man.
Point: If you can't change your product,
change your customers.

New business cards and a spruced up
website don't equate to REINVENTION.

The only thing more painful than changing

your brand is watching your business

die a slow death.

What is your business doing today that will make

it substantively different in the eyes

of your customers tomorrow?

REINVENTION

Tomorrow doesn't care whether you exist or not.

Consolidations and mergers are business decisions, but not necessarily brand REINVENTION.

Johnny Carson told Steve Martin, "To be successful (in show biz), you'll use everything you've ever learned." But isn't that the case in EVERY business? To REINVENT, employ every tool in your toolbox!

BE AN OBSERVER, RATHER THAN A COPIER. OBSERVERS SEE TRENDS TO PROFIT FROM TOMORROW, COPYCATS SEE WHAT WORKED YESTERDAY.

Three reasons REINVENTION doesn't happen: too lazy to change, fear of change, or arrogance that you're so good you don't need to change.

There are no replays in life and business, but there is REINVENTION.

If you still describe yourself by saying, "In high school I was...." Stop it. The only people who care what you were in high school are your classmates still living out their teenage years.

Don't mistake your fear-induced

paralysis for caution.

One idea can spawn your business.

Fresh ideas will keep you IN business.

The successful constantly

transform to today's environment.

HAPPY, SUCCESSFUL PEOPLE DON'T LIVE IN THE PAST.

The worst thing you can do to a new idea is tell un-inventive people about it.

You can either take the necessary, sometimes difficult steps of transformation, or you can complain and reminisce about the good old days.

A unicorn won't appear in a magic puff of smoke and haul you to a prosperous tomorrow. Change is up to you.

REINVENTION

Dinosaurs didn't have a choice about REINVENTING themselves. You do.

Success and longevity require continuous creativity because what seemed novel yesterday is soon antiquated.

Innovators study customer trends and current events to fill the void in tomorrow's marketplace.

Vision means seeing how you and your business successfully occupy the future.

Most people never take a risk or push themselves to the edge, then call those who did "lucky."

99% of all species that have ever roamed the Earth are extinct. Over 50% of businesses don't make it 5 years. Point? In nature and in business, extinction is the rule, not the exception.

REINVENTION

They say in life there are no re-rides.

But they never said you couldn't REINVENT yourself and do it over differently.

Most businesses won't REINVENT themselves, and that's a golden opportunity for the rest of us!

Let me get this straight, you're going to do the same thing this year as last year, yet you expect a different result?

NOBODY

CARES

HOW GOOD

YOU USED

TO BE!

IT'S NOT EASY BEING
A TRUTH TELLER

As high school class president, he was nearly banned from delivering a commencement address out of fear he'd "be too harsh." In corporate America, his candor was reprimanded in a "yes man" PC culture.

From the principal's office to the human resources office, people attempted to censor Damian's brutal truth. Lucky for you, it didn't work.

Today, Damian delivers honest insights laced with heavy doses of humor at corporate meetings all over North America.

CONTACT INFO

If you'd like to hire Damian Mason to speak at your next event, or to obtain any of his materials:

www.damianmason.com

888-304-0702

f /DamianMasonProfessionalSpeaker

🐦 @DamianPMason

in DamianMason